XL MACHINES!

CHERRY PICKERS

SETH KINGSTON

New York

Published in 2020 by The Rosen Publishing Group, Inc.
29 East 21st Street, New York, NY 10010

First Edition

Editor: Greg Roza
Book Design: Michael Flynn

Photo Credits: Cover, p. 1 ewg3D/iStock/Getty Images; series background (dirt) exopixel/Shutterstock.com; p. 5 Juan Enrique del Barrio/Shutterstock.com; p. 7 K Goldsmith/Shutterstock.com; p. 9 Askolds Berovskis/Shutterstock.com; p. 11 (telescopic arm) Lloyd Paulson/Shutterstock.com; p. 11 (scissor lift) anmbph/Shutterstock.com; p. 13 Mayura Ladaeng/Shutterstock.com; p. 15 Sergey Ryzhov/Shutterstock.com; p. 17 Roman023_photography/Shutterstock.com; p. 19 Phil Lowe/Shutterstock.com; p. 21 David Davies/PA Images/Getty Images; p. 22 3DMAVR/Shutterstock.com.

Cataloging-in-Publication Data

Names: Kingston, Seth.
Title: Cherry pickers / Seth Kingston.
Description: New York : PowerKids Press, 2020. | Series: XL machines! | Includes glossary and index.
Identifiers: ISBN 9781725311428 (pbk.) | ISBN 9781725311442 (library bound) | ISBN 9781725311435 (6pack)
Subjects: LCSH: Cherry pickers (Machines)–Juvenile literature.
Classification: LCC TJ1363.K56 2020 | DDC 621.8'73–dc23

Manufactured in the United States of America

CPSIA Compliance Information: Batch #CSPK19. For Further Information contact Rosen Publishing, New York, New York at 1-800-237-9932.

CONTENTS

Way Up There!

A cherry picker is a machine that lifts workers into the air. This lets them reach high places. Both the truck that includes the machine and the machine itself may be called cherry pickers. You've probably seen cherry pickers around your community. They're used for many jobs!

Picking Cherries

In 1944, a man named Jay Eitel spent a summer picking cherries. He spent a lot of time climbing a ladder, moving the ladder, and climbing it again. This led Eitel to create a machine he called a cherry picker! It had a **platform** that lifted workers into the air.

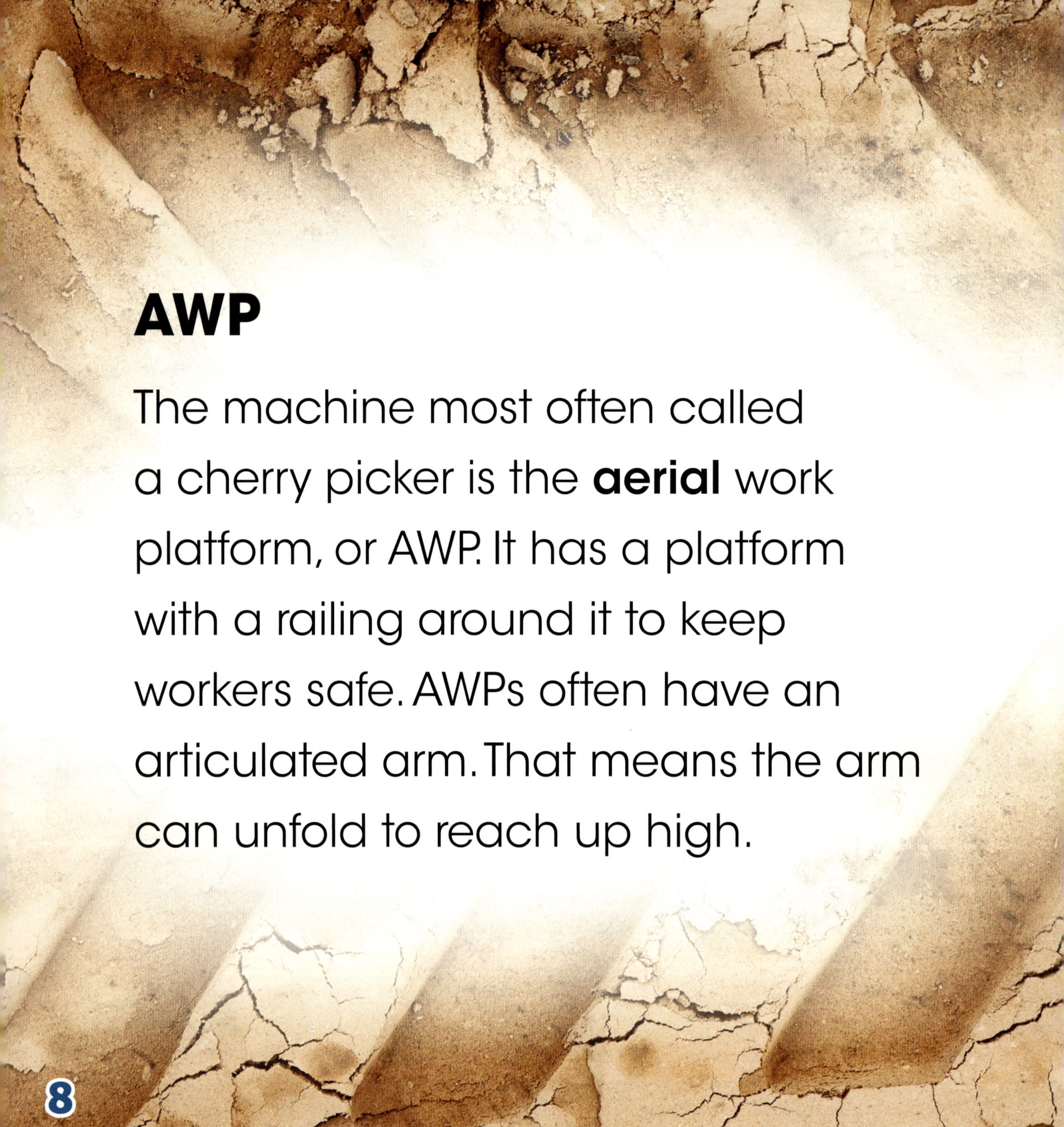

AWP

The machine most often called a cherry picker is the **aerial** work platform, or AWP. It has a platform with a railing around it to keep workers safe. AWPs often have an articulated arm. That means the arm can unfold to reach up high.

Telescopes and Scissors

Some cherry pickers have a telescopic arm. That means the arm has pieces that fit and move together to get longer or shorter. Other cherry pickers are called scissor lifts because the lifting part works like a pair of scissors. Scissor lifts can only go straight up and straight down.

scissor lift

telescopic arm

Getting Around

Small cherry pickers can be pushed into place. Some are moved on a trailer. Others are **mounted** on a truck. Some cherry pickers can be driven, just like people drive cars. They have **controls** in the **bucket**. Workers can raise and lower the bucket and even drive around.

F1
F2
F3
F4
F5
TEST
MENU

Put Down the Feet

Cherry pickers have a wide, heavy base so they don't tip over. Some have strong wheels or tracks. Many cherry pickers have extra "feet." Workers lower the feet so they rest on the ground. This keeps the cherry picker from falling over. It also keeps workers safe.

Build It Higher!

Cherry pickers are a common sight at **construction** sites. They're used to help build tall buildings. Workers use them to fix windows and paint walls that are high up. Workers use them to lift heavy supplies. Smaller cherry pickers are used to paint rooms, put in lights, and more.

Trouble!

Cherry pickers are often used to help people. Storms can knock down power lines and telephone wires. Workers use cherry pickers to fix them. Some fire trucks have cherry pickers. Firefighters sometimes use them to reach people trapped in tall buildings.

STREET
CLOSED

Other Uses

Picking fruit is still one of the most common uses for cherry pickers. They can be found on many orchards, or tree farms. Some companies use cherry pickers to trim tall trees. Cherry pickers are also used for filming movies and sporting events.

EPL Skylift

Even Higher!

The Bronto F112HLA is the tallest truck-mounted cherry picker in the world. The articulated arm can reach up to 367 feet (112 m) high! This giant cherry picker has been used to build roller coasters, wind farms, and radio towers. Workers can reach places 33 floors above the ground!

GLOSSARY

aerial: Having to do with being high in the air.

bucket: The container on a cherry picker a worker might stand in. They are usually round and have tall sides.

construction: Having to do with the act of building something.

control: A part of a machine that allows a person to make it work.

mount: To fix something on top of something else.

platform: A flat, raised surface for people to stand on.

INDEX

WEBSITES

Due to the changing nature of Internet links, PowerKids Press has developed an online list of websites related to the subject of this book. This site is updated regularly. Please use this link to access the list: www.powerkidslinks.com/xlm/cherrypickers